Business Coach Secrets

Be a Highly Effective Business Coach That Gets Tons of High Paying Clients

Christian Mickelsen

Christian Mickelsen

Christian@CoachesWithClients.com

San Diego, CA

(800) 492-7152

Limits of Liability and Disclaimer of Warranty

The author and publisher shall not be liable for your misuse of this material. This book is strictly for informational and educational purposes.

Warning – Disclaimer

The purpose of this book is to educate and entertain. The author and/or publisher do not guarantee that anyone following these techniques, suggestions, tips, ideas, or strategies will become successful. The author and/or publisher shall have neither liability nor responsibility to anyone with respect to any loss or damage caused, or alleged to be caused, directly or indirectly, by the information contained in this book.

ISBN-13: 978- 1728619910

TABLE OF CONTENTS:

CHAPTER 1

Business Coaching: The Opportunity Of A Lifetime

CHAPTER 2

3 Secrets To Make Big Money As A Business Coach

CHAPTER 3

The 4 Levels Of Value You Can Create For Clients

CHAPTER 4

The 5 Keys To Becoming A Big Money Business Coach

CHAPTER 5

The 3 Steps For Getting Business Owner Clients

CHAPTER 6

How To Get All The Business Owner Clients You Want

CHAPTER 7

5 Strategies That'll Help Your Clients Make Big Money Fast

ABOUT THE AUTHOR

CHAPTER 1
Business Coaching: The Opportunity Of A Lifetime!

Many years ago, in the early days of my coaching business, I was having a really down day.

I was really doubting myself, wondering if I was good enough to really be a coach and help people.

I ended up getting a call, and I didn't take it.

I checked my voicemail, and it was a call from Forbes Magazine.

They had found my website, and they wanted to ask me questions about coaching.

They left me a voicemail with the questions they wanted answered.

At the time I thought to myself, "You know what? I'm feeling bad today.

I'm just going to wait and call them back tomorrow."

But then I told myself, "Well, they're not interviewing me because I'm famous. They're interviewing me just because they want some answers and they think I might have them, but they might just find some other people to ask questions of."

So, I thought, "I better muster up some energy and call them back."

I answered all their questions, and I asked them if they would put my website in the article and put a link to it.

The guy said, "You know, we can't link it, but maybe we could list it."

I said, "Well, what's your email address? I'll email you some backup info that you wanted to know about coaching and once the article comes out, you can let me know about it and I can tell everybody about it."

I, once again, asked him if he would list my website in the article.

I told him that the website wasn't finished yet, but it was going to be ready any day.

When I first asked him, there was nothing at the URL. It was a completely dead URL. But, I asked him anyway, which was pretty bold.

Then, all of a sudden, I started getting emails from people I knew including past clients that I had worked with based on an article on Yahoo! Finance.

I was like, "Yahoo! Finance, they must be confused because I got interviewed by Forbes."

But, the article got picked up by Yahoo! Finance and ended up being on MSN, and, of course, it was on Forbes.

All that exposure got lots of people reaching out to me for coaching.

It didn't explode my business and turn me into an overnight success or anything like that, but it definitely was a nice blip for my business.

It helped me get a bunch of new clients, and, of course, gave me some extra credibility to say, "Hey, I was seen on forbes.com," and it worked out great.

The point of the story is that if you wait until you have it all figured out, if you wait until you're ready, you could miss out on some great opportunities.

I could have missed out on that Forbes interview.

I could have missed that extra publicity, the extra clients, the extra money, the extra revenue, and the extra feather in my cap of having had that experience.

It all starts from being bold, taking risks, betting on yourself, going for it.

That's why I wrote this book. Becoming a highly paid business coach has allowed me to live an amazing lifestyle.

And now, it's my goal to help as many people as possible to be bold and follow in my footsteps.

I Love Having A Coaching Business, And I Love Helping People

I love how appreciative all my clients are.

I love when they have success, and they call and leave me a voicemail and celebrate with me.

I also love when they post in our Facebook groups and tell me how they're succeeding.
That's one of my greatest joys in doing what I get to do.

I also get to put on all these seminars and have lots of people come.

I get to hang out with really cool people and get great speaking opportunities to speak on a lot of big stages.

The side effect is I make tons of money, and I get to live the greatest lifestyle.

I get to work as much or as little as I want. I get to spend lots of time with my girls.

I get to have lots of family time. I get to travel as much as I want and I usually only work part-time.

I've been able to grow my business to over $5,000,000 a year. I've made the Inc. 5000 List of Fastest Growing Companies for the last three years in a row.

So, I know how to grow a business right now, today in this environment with modern technology and social media.

Not only have I been able to grow my own business to multi-millions, I've coached a lot of other business owners, and I've been able to help coach them to super high levels of success too.

That's what I want to show you how to do inside of this book.

You're going to discover how to be a highly effective business coach that gets tons of high paying clients.
You'll also discover five ways to help business owner clients make big money fast.

Best part?

These are strategies that you can use for your own business as well!

These are the same strategies I've discovered over 18+ years as a highly-paid business coach where I routinely get paid $100,000+ for a consulting day.

But I have a small confession for you:

I Wasn't Born With A Silver Spoon In My Mouth

My parents fought a lot, until they eventually divorced and my Dad left the house.

So my Mother raised 4 kids on a waitress's income and we grew up on welfare and food stamps.

She had to set us up on welfare programs: free lunches at school, food stamps, and food from a local food pantry.

We didn't always have enough money to pay utilities so there were times when we had to go without water, electricity, or garbage pick-up.

It was like playing musical chairs — never knowing which utility would be turned off next.

Not only that, but kids teased me about my ragged, old, out-of-style second hand clothes.

So, I definitely had some humble beginnings.

I eventually decided to become a coach when I was 25 years old.

I started off as a success coach and I coached people on all kinds of things—from weight loss to finding love, to career and then even business.

The problem is I struggled to get clients.

I was only charging $195 a month for a client, and the clients only signed up for a month.

Some of them lasted two months, three months, four months. Some lasted six months, but a lot of them only lasted a couple of months.

So I really struggled to pay my bills. I almost lost my house, many times, because I fell behind on my mortgage. I also fell behind on my car payments.

It got so bad I thought about quitting, many times and getting a full-time job.

In fact, I remember watching the garbage man pick up my trash one morning.

I thought to myself..."I would love to have a job like that right now! I won't have to think so hard, plus I will have a steady paycheck!"

Eventually, I was able to pick up five coaches who hired me to grow their business.

Four out of those first five coaches grew their business from zero to $100,000 within 18 months. One of them did it in 72 days.

That's when I realized, I get to share with other coaches what I've learned through the school of hard knocks—so they could have success even faster than I did.

Now today, I have a multimillion dollar coaching business. I work 20 hours a week, which is the perfect amount of time for me.

I also have a team of business coaches. We have 15 coaches on our team and 48 total employees.

I have an email list of over 300,000 business owners and over the years I've learned a ton about sales, marketing, leadership and coaching.

I'm one of the highest paid coaches on earth, with clients paying $100,000 to work with me for a single day.

I never even imagined that could be possible when I first got started.

In fact, I remember a few years into my coaching…
I remember somebody was charging $25,000 per year to work with their clients, and I thought to myself, Oh my God, one day I want to charge that much!"

It took me years to get myself to that point.

Eventually I got myself to a point where I was charging $100,000 for clients to work with me for a year.

I also have coaching and Mastermind groups where clients pay me up to $75,000 to work with me and my team for a year.

In fact, I actually won *Inc. Magazine's* award for being one of the 5000 fastest growing privately held companies in the U.S.

We did it for the last three years in a row. That's 2015, 2016, 2017 and this year has not been officially announced yet.

It feels great because I was not good at sports growing up. I never won any trophies other than the occasional participation trophy.

That's why it's a lot of fun to win trophies now!

And now I want to share all my strategies that took me year and millions of dollars to develop with you.

Why Being A Business Coach Is Awesome!
Business owners make great clients, because they're very success minded and ambitious, just like you.

You don't have to motivate them because they already want big success in their business.

They are also much more willing to invest in coaching. They understand the concept of spending money to make money.
They're more likely to invest $10,000 or $25,000, for example, if they know it'll make them an extra $100,000.

For them, it's a no-brainer.

For a coach looking for high-paying clients, this is like a dream come true.

Let's do the math real quick.

If you can get 25 clients that pay you $10,000 each (that's only just over 2 clients/month), that's $250,000 a year.

That's really good, because there's not a lot of overheads having a coaching business.

You don't even need to have an office.

Now let's do some more math.

You can even get 10 clients that pay $25,000 each (that's less than 1 client/month), and still make $250,000 a year.

You can really ramp things up and get 25 clients at $25,000 a year each, that's $625,000 a year.

That is a fantastic income!

Not only that, but you can become a business coach part-time if you already have a full-time job.

For example, just 3-4 clients at $10,000 to $25,000 each can create a decent side income for you.

So you don't have to get up and quit your job right away.
Plus coaching business owners doesn't require a lot of time, either.
You can easily transition into becoming a highly-paid business coach while you're at your current job.

So the possibilities are endless!
Not only that, but...

There Are 27.9 Million Small Business Owners In The Unites States (According To The U.S. Census Bureau)

You only need 15-20 of them to work with you during any given year to earn a massive income!

Plus the niche is exploding with a growth rate of 6%+ per year. And there's no signs of it slowing down anytime soon.

So there's plenty of opportunity out there to become a highly-paid business coach.

You just have to make the decision if you want to make the leap into the lucrative world of business coaching.

In the next chapter, I'm going to share the 3 secrets to make big money as a business coach most people don't talk about.

CHAPTER 2
The 3 Secrets To Make Big Money As A Business Coach

Many people think they need years of business experience and know sales and marketing like the back of their hand.

This cannot be further from the truth!

Here are 3 secrets to make big money as a business coach (some of these might surprise you!):

Secret #1: You Don't Need To Be Successful

You don't have to be a crazy successful superstar business owner with an incredible track record in order to help business owners.
People often think to themselves, "Why would a business owner hire me if I don't already have a million dollar business of my own? Why would anybody ever hire me to coach them on their million dollar business?"

There are actually a lot of reasons, and here are just some of them....

A) Your training, education and real world experiences are valuable assets

If you've had great training and you know some things that they don't, they're going to want to get your help on those things.

There's no limit to what these things can be, but if you've had training through school, special courses or on-the-job experience, there's a good chance that you know something that can benefit an owner's business.

B) Business owners need someone they can talk to

Another reason why business owners would hire a coach that isn't as successful as they are is because they just need someone they can talk to who will listen to them.

This is because a lot of times they can't talk to their friends and family about their problems, because the challenges that business owners face are unique to business owners.

In other words, most people just wouldn't understand.

Revenue targets, how much money the business is pulling in, and hiring and firing people are all challenges that are not relatable to family, friends, and employees.
So they need a good person that can support them and coach them through these unique challenges.

C) Coaching gives business owners clarity

The structure of coaching allows a business owner to communicate their problems and challenges out loud in a way that helps them see things that are difficult to see without a coach.

This one time I was coaching a business owner and it was one of our first sessions and I pulled out all the stops.

I was using my best ninja coaching techniques to work with him.

By the end of the session, I asked him what he found most valuable about our time together that day.

And he said "just hearing himself think."

Just being able to get all the things that were on his mind out of his head where he could see them and then do something about them was important.

Just being there for them, being somebody that they can talk to, in and of itself, is extremely valuable.

Secret #2: Business Owners Desperately Need Help

Most people think that business owners have it all figured out because there's an assumption that if they grew a successful business, they must be super smart and have it all together.

Well, here's a little secret...

There are a lot of business owners, even once they have million dollar businesses or multimillion dollar businesses, who are on the verge of burnout, or are on the verge of going out of business because they're not managing their cash flow.

Or, they don't have a great team growing the business for them.

I know several businesses with a lot of top line revenue, but didn't make a lot of profit, and then the business owner got burned out and just couldn't keep things going.
And even if the business is going well, there are always things that could be going better to keep the business growing.

That's another major area that you'll help with as a business coach. How to get more customers, how to hire better people, how to manage people, how to manage their time better.

These are all massive challenges for business owners.

The bottom line is that business owners don't have it all figured out and therein lies a massive opportunity for you to make big money.

Secret #3: Business Owners Are Willing To Pay More For Coaching

Hands down, the highest percentage of people willing to pay big money for coaching are owners.

Why?

1. There's already a high percentage of them just waiting to be coached
2. They understand that investing in coaching makes them more money.
3. They want to make more money and get more freedom and spend time with family, and great coaching can help them accomplish that.

Business owners have a lot invested in their business and they are willing to do much more than other types of clients to sustain success, get more success, and grow their businesses.

All you need to do is recognize this so you can start targeting high-paying business owner clients.
Next, we'll cover the 4 levels of value you can create for business owner clients.

Two of them may surprise you because they aren't directly involved with making money, but they're something business owners crave.

CHAPTER 3
The 4 Levels Of Value You Can Create For Clients

Now that we've reviewed the 3 secrets to make big money as a business coach, I'm going to share with you 4 levels of value you can create for clients.

These levels of value will help ensure that clients get massive benefits from your coaching and refer you to new clients in the process.

Value Level #1: Create the environment for coaching

The first level of value is just the environment of coaching itself.

Having them talk about what they want to achieve, their challenges and what actions they're going to take between now and their next session. If that's all you did every week from one session to the next, that's going to actually create a lot of value for clients because it gives them real and measurable goals to work on.

This creates positive momentum and inevitable results for your clients.

Value Level #2: Your personal experience

Chances are you have a background in sales or a background in management or leadership, or at the very least there's some experience that you can draw from to help you create value for your clients.

For example, the simple act of me growing my business to where it is today has allowed me to learn so much that I could turn around and offer it as value to my clients.

If all you did was build up your business, you're already gaining valuable experience that you can use to help others as well.

Value Level #3: Mindset and inner work

To be able to actually help people through their fears, their doubts, their limiting beliefs and their inner stuff that could be holding them back is an incredible value that you can create and offer to your clients.

In fact, this is one of the most valuable things you can do for your business owner clients and if you really love doing inner work with people, then business owners are one of the best groups of people to do the inner work with because

A) they appreciate it and
B) it will help them make a lot more money which will then help you be able to charge much more.

Value Level #4: Expertise

Another way to create massive value for business owner clients is through your expertise.

Expertise are the expert skills and knowledge you have in a particular field that you can help business owners with.

There may be specialized areas that you've studied such as sales or business. You may have gone to school for a particular field, or you may have taken a course on a specialized topic.

There's no limit to the kinds of expertise you can bring to the table, so whatever you've spent time learning can be ultra-valuable to business owners.

Next, we're going to cover 5 keys to becoming a Big Money Business Coach.

Implement all these keys and you'll be unstoppable!

CHAPTER 4
The 5 Keys To Becoming A Big Money Business Coach

Key #1: Help Them Create A Clear Vision

The first key to being a Big Money Business Coach is to help business owners create a clear vision for their business success...

...not just this year, but next year, over the next five years, over the next ten years, and beyond.

You can also help them create a strategic plan for how to get there.

Believe it or not, most business owners don't have a strategic plan.

And as the old saying goes, *"If you fail to plan, you plan to fail!"*
Even businesses that are "making it" don't have plans.

I know plenty of million dollar businesses out there that don't have a strategic plan.

They're just surviving when they could be thriving.

They just have a loose idea in their mind of what they need to focus on.

And this keeps business owners focused only on the short term.

They just focus on what's right in front of their nose, what they need to do right now today, or what they need to do this month.

It's like they're laying a train track while the train is already coming down the track!

They're trying to lay each piece of track right before the train comes onto that part of the track.

And then they're scrambling to try and get the next piece of track in front of them before the train derails.

They do this instead of building out the whole track ahead of time, so it's smooth sailing straight ahead.

Now, I'm not saying that business is always smooth sailing.

But, helping your clients create a strategic plan and a clear vision will definitely smooth out a lot of the bumps in the road.

Key #2: Help Them With Marketing

The second key to being a Big Money Business Coach is being able to help your clients create great marketing.

This starts with helping your clients identify their most profitable product or service.
Most businesses are focused on trying to sell to too many people.

And it's your job to help them narrow their focus like a laser beam.

You can have really diffused light that lights up a whole room, or you can have really focused light that burns a hole through a wall.

And when things are more narrow and more focused, they're more powerful and can create a lot more growth.

Key #3: Help Them With Sales

Whether they're struggling with sales or doing well, every business owner wants more!

You can evaluate how effective they are at getting sales and recommend alterative strategies they can implement in their business.

You can also help them find more customers so they can increase their revenue.

Many business owners are too busy on the day-to-day tasks in their business to recognize opportunities right under their nose.

You can be the one that gives them the breakthroughs they need to increase their sales.

That way, they can pay for your coaching over and over again, and never leave you!

Key #4: Help Your Clients With Leadership

The fourth key to being a Big Money Business Coach is to help your business owner clients hire a great team and be great leaders.

You see, the goal of true leadership is to build and lead a team that grows their business for them.
This frees up your client to think of new ideas for the business and to think ahead... which is something they're almost never doing.

And part of the reason they're not doing it is because they don't have a great team.

They haven't hired the right people and they haven't fired the people they should've fired a long time ago.

Also, they probably don't have a great team culture.

They may have a lot of turnover where people are coming and going a lot.

So they're always busy hiring new people.

This is distracting them from things that make the most money, like strategic planning, creating a vision, and sales & marketing.

When you can help them do these things as a Big Money Business Coach, you become an extremely valuable asset.

That's why paying you $10,000, $25,000, or even $100,000 or more to work together is a no brainer.

But, it won't be an easy "YES" for these high-paying clients to hire you if you don't have a great sales and marketing process of your own.

That's why I'll be sharing my time-tested and proven marketing system with you when you decide to join the Big Money Business Coach training and certification program.

Key #5: Help Clients Master Their Psychology

Finally, the fifth key to becoming a Big Money Business Coach is helping clients master their mindset, or master their psychology.

You see, business owners are dealing with all kinds of inner insecurities. Maybe, they have insecurities with their team.

They may think, "Oh my God this person on my team is so much smarter than I am."

They also may be worried that other people on their team are going to realize they're not as smart as they are.

Maybe they want bigger clients of their own, but they're afraid to go talk to those big clients because they feel intimidated.

Maybe they have negative beliefs about money that prevent them from raising their fees.

There's so many negative thoughts going on in a business owner's head that could keep them from making progress.

And the more we can help business owners get all that stuff cleared out, the more they can be peaceful and centered and at their best.

That way, they can do their best work and their best planning.

So, those are the 5 keys to becoming a Big Money Business Coach.

Next, we're going to cover 3 steps to getting business owner clients to hire you.

| 29

CHAPTER 5
The 3 Steps To Getting Business Owner Clients

Now that we've talked about the 5 keys to becoming a Big Money Business Coach, we're now going to talk about how to get business owner clients to hire you.

Step #1: Get them to hear about you.

The first step to get business owner clients that pay big is to get them to hear about you.

And, fortunately, this is much easier than most people think.

Like I mentioned earlier in this book, there are 27.8 million small businesses in the US alone.

That's a lot of potential clients!

We'll cover where you can find these business owner clients later in this book, but for now, know this:

If business owners don't know who you are, and if they don't hear anything about you, it's going to be tricky to get clients.

You need to get in front of your ideal prospects and establish yourself as an expert and show them what you can do.

One way to do that is the instant credibility formula which I'll share with you right now. This incredible formula looks like this...

1. Speak Simply And Clearly
2. Speak The Language Of Clients
3. Teach Them Something Valuable

So let's dive into each step!

Speak Simply And Clearly

There was a study done several years ago to find out what makes an expert witness credible to a jury.

They did numerous studies to find out what kind of people have the most credibility...

- Is it because the person has a PhD? Is that what makes them seem credible? *No.*
- Is it the extensive research that they've done, does that make them credible? *Still, no.*
- Was it all the years of experience they had? Did that make them credible? *Again, no.*

So if it wasn't any of these things, then what made people the most credible?

It was the person who spoke the clearest and simplest, and who was the easiest to understand!

That was the person that was more believable. Not just more understandable, but more believable.

The person who communicated their ideas the simplest and clearest was the person that the jury believed was the better expert than the one who had all the credentials.

The reason I share this with you is because most coaches out there don't believe in themselves, simply because they don't have a fancy title or lots of credentials.

But as you can see, these things are not the most important.
What's really important is that you can articulate clearly and simply so that anyone can understand you.

When you do this, you've already taken care of one of the major keys to instant credibility.

And here's the next...

Speak The Language Of Clients

You have to speak the language of clients, which is the language of results.

In other words you need to talk about what they care about.
Let me give you an example.

I was working with one of my $75,000 Mastermind clients recently.

She's a weight loss coach, actually, but all of her marketing was about her system for helping people get results -- all of her marketing was so beautiful.

The copy was good, but the target was off, because she wasn't actually talking about the result that people wanted directly.

She wasn't talking about getting thinner, losing weight, getting slim.

She was talking about helping people with her system that would end up getting them thin.

She wasn't focusing right on the "getting thin" part.

People don't care about how, they care about what.

Eventually they'll want to know how, but you've got to get their attention with the what.

You lead with the what... which is the result they're after!

Here's another example:

Let's say you're coaching business owners who have a medical practice.

If you say things like, "Hey, let's grow your practice," you're now speaking their language.

You're talking about getting more patients and generating more money.

What you want to avoid is statements like, "eliminate stress".
A statement like this needs to be more specific because stress is just a part of business.

Stress doesn't just wash off like dirt with water.

You want to talk about the specific results to the problems that people have out there.

The problems that business owners have and the results they're looking for.

If you can describe what a business owner's problem is better than they can, then they automatically assume that you have the solution.

So, what to do business owners care about?

They care about growing their business, sales, profits, getting more customers, and getting more clients.

They also care about Increasing profit margins, growing their team, and getting their team to grow their business for them.

If we start talking about that, a bell will go off in their head that goes, "Ding, ding, ding! I'll have some of that!"

You also want to talk about the things that are frustrating to them, their challenges, and their struggles.

That includes what it's like to have your own business, having things grow, and having things shrink occasionally.

You can talk to them about having a good month, having a bad month, having problems with your team, having a key person on your team quit or having a bunch of people on your team quit all at once.

The latter is the ultimate nightmare for any business owner!

Now the biggest problem most business owners have is not having enough customers. Then, the second biggest problem people have is having too many customers.
When you have too many customers, you need your team to be able to handle all the infrastructure.

Once you've gotten in front of your ideal clients, your next step is to teach them something valuable.

That's basically what I'm doing right here. I'm showing you that I'm an expert by teaching you stuff that's valuable.

That includes things that you can use immediately to start growing your business and help get more clients for you.

The better I can do that in this book, the more I think that you'll trust me, that you'll want to keep learning from me.

Maybe you'll even become one of my next $100,000 clients!

So how do you choose your ideal clients?

There are a lot of ways. I like working with business owners of all sorts. But eventually I started focusing more on helping coaches, just because so many coaches were wanting my help.

I like working with business owners of all sorts, but you can pick a niche.

For example, there's a lot of money in coaching dentists, doctors, chiropractors, plumbers or printing companies.

Specializing is great too. There are a lot of ways to specialize.

You can specialize by a business niche or you could specialize by business topic.

You could teach a specific piece of business success (such as growing sales) and become known for that.

Teach Them Something Valuable

When you teach someone something valuable, they're very likely to remember you and respect you a lot more.

Sure, you can talk about your accolades, but that's not nearly as effective as proving that you know your profession through giving real value.

When you can teach something valuable right off the bat, you'll have people say things like "Hey, you know what, if your free stuff is this good then your paid stuff is probably even better."

In summary...

The first way to create instant credibility is to speak simply and clearly.

It's not about best-selling books, PhDs, or famous clients and amazing testimonials.

Those things are helpful but the most important thing is; speak simply and clearly.

Be articulate.

Number two, talk about the things your clients care about.

Speak their language. Growing their business, making more money, working less hours.

Talk about the pains, problems and challenges they're going through and be specific.

Then number three, teach them something valuable.

If you can do those three things, then you can have instant credibility with your perspective clients.

Step #2: Get them to have an introductory session with you.

This is how you get business owner clients to hire you. Obviously it needs to be done effectively.

You need to run these introductory sessions so business owners will get out their credit card and buy right on the spot.

You need to know what to do when people say they want to talk to their spouse, or they want to talk to their business partner.

You also need to be able to talk about your coaching fees and transition to the offer in a way that makes them excited and not defensive.

Sometimes, people detect when an offer is coming and they're like, "Oh yikes!"

They start getting defensive because they think you're trying to like be pushy or manipulative.

One of the things I teach is to reverse pressure.

You do that by pulling away the pressure over and over again until you've created a gap. That way, the prospective client keeps moving toward you.

Then you step back again and then they step towards you again.

Anyway, you need to be able to do it in a way that doesn't make people put up their defenses.

You want to make sure that the prospective client feels like you are on their side trying to help them...instead of being just another sale for you.

You want to be able to close the sale with zero pressure, and an eager "Yes!"

Step #3: Get Hired!

Obviously you want to make it easy for them to pay you with their credit card. You may even do wire transfers. PayPal even works along with checks.

You want to use magic phrases that make them feel comfortable and confident to give you their credit card right over the phone.

And of course, then you need to coach them incredibly well so they're super happy, they stick around forever, and they refer lots of people to you.

So that's the three-step process for getting high-paying business owner clients.

This process is great because it streamlines a lot of things.

Why? Because many people focus their time and energy on things that don't make them money.

For example, many people are spending hours and hours on social media.

I'm not saying social media can't be an effective strategy to grow your brand, to grow your presence, to grow your following, and become an influencer.

Those things can be valuable, but it's really easy to take your eyes off the prize and realize that it can be as easy as this 3 step process:

1. People hear about you
2. They have a session with you
3. They hire you

Plus a lot of people think, "My gosh, people need to hear about us eight thousand times before they'll trust us. They need to see our ad a million times before they'll respond to it…"

There may be some truth to that, especially if you're doing mass marketing offers.
But for the kind of things that you and I do, results can be quicker.

You could meet someone at a networking event and sign them up as a client the same day.

You could post something on social media and (if you do it the right way) get people to sign up to have a free session with you.

Then you can sign them up as a client the same day, or later that week.

Next, we're going to cover how to get all the business owner clients you want.

CHAPTER 6
How To Get All The Business Owner Clients You Want!

So how do you get business owner clients?

The good news is you interact with businesses all the time. Not necessarily the owner, but you interact with businesses all the time.

Every time you go to a restaurant, every time you go to a store, and any time you buy something on the internet, you interact with a business.

You could just ask to meet with the owner. If the owner isn't there, you could ask, "when is the owner going to be here?"

This may seem crazy, but one of my clients did this.

She would just go walk into a businesses and ask to speak to the owner, and then get to know them a little bit.

She would ask them a few questions, and see if they wanted to set up a free coaching session.

And then during that free session, she would then sign them up, and turn them into clients.

That's not to say this is the most effective method, but it's an option.

Outside of simply walking into a business and asking for the owner, here are some examples of places you could find business owner clients so they hear about you:

Local Networking Events

There are lots of local networking events in most places around the world because business owners like connecting with other business owners.

It's an effective way to do business and get clients.

For example, if someone is a business attorney and someone else is a business accountant and they become friends, there's a huge potential for both of them to get new clients.

That's because all the business attorney's clients might need an accountant, and all the accountant's clients might need a business attorney.

And both of those people can refer clients to a business coach like yourself.

This is just one simple example of why networking events are a great way to go meet other business owners and potentially get clients.

Business Development Seminars

Another great place to get clients is at business development seminars.

There are lots of seminars all over the world where business owners attend to learn how to run their business.

These people are prime prospects for your business because you know they are already looking for help, since they are at the seminar.

So the stage is essentially set for you.
From there, it's a matter of having a quality conversation and offering to have an intro session.

I remember when I was 26 years old and wanted to pick up more business owner clients.

So, I went to a ½ day business development seminar.
I went there because I wanted to network, but I was dismayed to find out the person who was leading it was another business coach.

I thought to myself, "This is a waste of me coming to this event as a way to get clients,"

Why?

Because I didn't realize the person who taught it was a business coach.

I just thought nobody in this room would hire me after hearing from this guy!

But I ended up chatting with somebody after the workshop was over.

He was excited and said, "Man, you know, can I take you to lunch, because I'd love to learn more about what you do!"

So, he took me to lunch.

At lunch, I took them through a process that I teach for signing up clients, which is called Free Sessions That Sell: The Client Sign Up System.

And he signed up to hire me right on the spot.

So I ended up getting a client at another business coach's workshop!

Social Media Groups

Another big place to find business owner clients is in social media groups. For example, Facebook or LinkedIn groups that target business owners.

Your goal in social media groups is to be as helpful as possible every time you interact with someone. Or, you could offer a resource to members of a particular community to get them on your email list. This will lead them to get on the phone with you, which sets the stage for you to get hired easily.

Social Media Ads

This is different than the social media groups described above because it's paid advertisement.

One of the best ways to attract business owner clients is with Facebook ads or social media ads.

LinkedIn ads could potentially be great too because it's easier to find people who market themselves as a CEO.

You can then send ads to people who fit that or any other category, who self-select themselves as their job.

When you do that, you can target people in your local area and invite them to a local workshop you're doing, or you can just send them to a website, and say "we're offering a video or a free special report."

Ads are great because they are direct and fast.

Guest Blogging And Being A Guest On Podcasts

These can give you major exposure if you do it right.

Blogs and podcasts are always looking for special guests to write a guest blog or be a guest on their show, respectively.

These also give you major credibility, because if you're a guest on a major blog or podcast, then you must really know what you're talking about.

Offer A Helpful Resource

Once you get in front of people then you'll want to want to offer some sort of a resource to help them out. This kind of resource will help get people on your email list, for example.
You could offer them a free video training, a free article or a free tele-class or a free webinar. Those are some of the things that you could offer that could make them want to go from initial conversation to getting on your email list.

And one of the best things that you could offer as an incentive to get on your email list is a free business assessment.

People like to assess themselves and they like to find out more about what's going on with them. And for business owners, they would love a scorecard to see how they are stack up in their business.

In my Big Money Business Coach program, I actually have three assessments that we use to help different types of clients.

1. One for business owner clients
2. One for leadership and executive clients
3. And one for sales professionals.

All three of these assessments are great tools to get people on your email list because it shows them the gaps and how far they need to go. This is super valuable and interesting for business owners to know about themselves.

Business Owner Assessment

Below I'm giving you the business assessment now at no charge.
This is my gift to you.

Take this assessment and use it. It could be something that you give away
for people to get on your email list or a resource that you can offer to
people that could be really helpful.

If you do a live workshop or webinar or a live tele-class, it's also a tool that
you can administer live during your webinar or tele-class.

The great thing about this assessment is that it's a self-assessment, so it's
their own answers.

They put in for themselves what they feel is true.

It's not you telling them, "Hey, you know what, your marketing isn't doing
great." It's them saying, "Oh, my marketing is not that great."

They can't argue with themselves. If they have scales from 1 to 10, and they
give themselves a five or less on any of these 7 or 10 categories, they've got
work to do.
They can try doing it on their own or they can do it with your help.

One question I'll ask you is, is it easier for them to have success by
themselves or would it be easier for them to be successful with your help?

My belief is, if they do it on their own – it's MUCH more difficult.

And that's why you're here. They need your help. So let's get people
coached!

Rapid Business Growth:
BUSINESS OWNER ASSESSMENT

Use this special assessment to identify your greatest leverage points for rapid growth.

On a scale from 0-10, please rate your business in the following areas...

_____ I have a crystal clear vision for where my business is headed

_____ I have a specific, step-by-step plan for how to achieve all of my business goals

_____ I have a powerful support team that is filled with "A" players only

_____
_____ When it comes to building my team, "I dig my well, before I'm thirsty," meaning I always look ahead for the next people to add to my team before I need them

_____ I'm aware of industry trends, economic trends, and technology trends that will impact the future of my business and we're poised to capitalize on these trends

_____ I have marketing strategies that work effectively

_____ I always test and measure the results of every marketing activity we implement so that we can constantly improve our results

_____ I have a systemized sales process that ensures my sales team members can all be successful

_____ I have a system in place for rewarding my team regularly in ways that they love to be rewarded (praise, gifts, public acknowledgement)

_____ I keep my eyes on our business financial reports and safeguard our cash flow

CHAPTER 7
Five Strategies That'll Help Your Clients Make Big Money Fast

Like I mentioned earlier in this book, *many business owners are struggling.*

That's one thing I've discovered after I started working with business owners 18 years ago.

A lot of them are struggling and it was a challenge for them to afford me.

This was the case even when I wasn't charging all that much in the early days of my coaching business.

They needed to make money and they needed it fast.

And I needed to figure out how I could help them make money fast, so they could boost their cashflow.

Why Getting Fast Results For Your Clients Is Critical

When you can get your clients results quickly, they're more likely to listen to you and follow your lead on those long-term strategies.

When someone is paying you money, they're going to be very open to listening to what you have to say.

They'll be more likely to take your advice and at least give it a shot.

They're also more likely to try your strategies a second or third time if the first time doesn't pan out.

That's why the faster you can get them results, the better (we'll discuss how to do that later in this book).

If you can get to help them make quick money right away, they will now listen to you and trust you more.

They'll also be open in investing with you at higher and higher fees because you've proved you know your stuff.

Plus, if they can make enough money in the first 30, 60 or even 90 days, it'll pay for the whole year of coaching.

That way, you don't have to worry about whether they're going to be dropping out partway through the year.

It makes your business more stable because you're not constantly hustling to get new clients to replace the ones that dropped out.

Of course, you ideally want to get clients to pay in full upfront, which we'll talk about later in this book.

In fact, this is what I teach in my coaching programs.

We teach people to get their clients to pay up front. This is much better than having them on a payment plan.

Of course, payment plans are great.

If somebody is on a payment plan and now they're crushing it and making a lot of money, what are the chances that they're going to stick around, make all their payments and be a great client for you?
Much, much higher, right?

So, that's another reason why helping business owner clients make money fast is critical

So here are 5 "fast money" strategies you can use to help your clients make so much money in the first month, that they'll keep you around forever!

Fast Money Strategy #1: Do More Of What's Working Best

There are so many great ideas and so many products to sell for a typical business owner.

It's really easy to lose track of what is actually making the money.

Here's an example.

When Steve Jobs took over Apple, they had a 120+ products they were selling, and he narrowed it down to just eight.

So, when you're working with business owners, help them figure out where they are making most of their money.

Here's an example from my own business:

We have 40+ different online training programs. But I found that it was really difficult to try to sell 40+ programs.

But then we looked at the programs that made the most money.

And most of the money was made through two programs. So we decided to focus on those programs.

The 80/20 rule says that 80% of our results come from 20% of our efforts. So, how can you get your business owner clients to do more of the good stuff and less of the fluff?

Here are some power questions to ask your business owner clients.

— Where do you make most of your money?
— What's your best-selling product or service?
— What are your best source of leads?

You see, a lot of people get overwhelmed when it comes to lead sources.

They think to themselves they have to do Facebook, social media, etc...to get more leads.

So, how many do you actually need?

The truth is you only need one lead source you can execute really well. Now, I'm not saying you should only do one, but sometimes the other ones can be a big distraction.

So get your business owner clients to double down and focus on:

— Their best source of leads
— Their bestselling product
— Their highest-converting ad
— Their best joint-venture partners
— Their highest value customer.

This could give them an immediate profit windfall that'll more than pay for your coaching!

Fast Money Strategy #2: Re-activate Past Clients

Re-activating past clients is often a gold mine just sitting there, waiting to be found.

Why?

Because most people ignore their past clients or customers, because they're so focused on generating new leads and selling to new customers.

So a great question to ask your business owner clients is this:

"What can you do to activate your past customers?"

It's often way faster and easier to get an old customer to buy again, than to go out and find a brand new customer.

I remember when I started my first group coaching program. I had been coaching for three years at the time.

So I had several one-on-one clients I had worked with for various lengths of time.

I reached out to my past one-on-one clients to see if they were interested, and many of them jumped in.

This was the first time I launched a group coaching program.

And all I had to do was simply contact my past clients to see if they wanted to join. And a lot of them said "Yes."

So, here are some power questions to ask business owner clients:

1. Can you create a special offer just for your past clients?
2. Can you just simply reach out to them and see if they're ready for more of what you offer?
3. Can you create something new for these clients?

Fast Money Strategy #3: Go Back To What Worked In The Past

So many times we do something in our businesses and it's working really well.

And then, for some reason, we stop doing it.

Maybe we get too busy with our current clients.

This happens to a lot of people, especially solopreneurs.

They work really hard to market, market, market, and then they get a bunch of clients and ignore marketing.

Then, they just work with those clients, they get the revenue, and then some of the clients leave them.

All of a sudden their income drops and they have to market themselves again.

And then they forget, "Well, now what do I do to get more clients?"

They forget what they did that worked so well.

Maybe they just did a lot of things, and they weren't keeping track of what worked the best to get the clients in the past.
So, a lot of people aren't even aware of what's working best, which is why it's so important to ask those questions right away.

But it's easy to get busy with current clients, or maybe you get some ideas and you get distracted.

This used to be one of my biggest angsts I had in my business.

I would just get idea, after idea, after idea. Then, I would write them down so I could act on them.

And then I was thinking to myself, "My God!" I would get so overwhelmed.

Eventually, I just surrendered to the idea.

First I thought, "All right, even if I don't act on them, I'll just make sure I write them all down."

Eventually, I just decided, "You know what, it doesn't matter if I write them down or not.

There are a million other million dollar ideas waiting where that one came from. I don't need to write down all my ideas."

Just let them in and let them go.

And if one keeps calling me strong enough, then eventually it's going to get my attention and get me to take action.

But, it's easy to get distracted and never get back on track.

You'd be surprised how many people get away from things that are working really well.

For example, I actually had a program that was selling like hotcakes.

Then, I got a new idea for a new program, and I launched the other program, and I never went back to selling that original hot seller.

As a result, sales went down and didn't recover for nine months.

That's because I didn't stick with what was already working for me.

Now I'm in a place where I pay much closer attention to all the numbers I've kept.

Like I said earlier in this book, I have almost 50 people on my team.
So, I have to keep an eye on all sorts of things that I didn't necessary have to keep an eye on before.

But these kind of things happen to business owners all the time.

So a good question to ask your business owner clients is this:

"What have you done in the past that worked really well for getting clients or for growing your business that you aren't doing right now? And why not?"

This question should get your business owner clients back to what worked in the past, and on the road to making fast money.

Fast Money Strategy #4: The Big Sale

This is something that can lead to an immediate profit windfall for your clients.

To maximize this strategy, you're going to want to make a big discount.
I recommend creating a big sale somewhere in the range of 50% to 80% off.
It has to be something drastic in order to get people's attention.

Plus, a lot of businesses have dead inventory. These are things that aren't going to sell.

And a lot of times business owners are afraid to sell that at a discount, because they feel like they're going to lose money.

Maybe they buy something for a $100. They buy something for a $100, and then the goal would be to sell it for $200.

Then it doesn't sell, and then maybe they even put on a sale. But they would still try to break even.

They think to themselves, "Well, if I sell it for less, then I lose money on it. If I bought it for $100 and now I sell it for $50, I'm going to lose that money."

And they don't want to lose that money.

The problem is it's never going to sell!

So, it's much better to get $50 back out of the 100, then to get zero back.

This is one of those strategies where a business owner needs to make big money fast.

Just blow out that old inventory.

Finally, you want to give people a deadline when it comes to your big sale.

Urgency and scarcity are huge motivators.

An example of this is to have a 50% off sale for just 48-72 hours.
We as coaches think it's so weird to put things on sale sometimes, but what percentage of the time do you think clothes at a clothing store is on sale?

A lot, but it depends on the store. For example, I remember the first time I walked in Bloomingdales. I noticed a T-shirt was $100-$300.

I thought to myself, "Forget that! This place is insane. I would never shop there."

And then I got a lot richer, and then I walked back in, and I thought to myself, "Dang, that is a really nice T-shirt."

Almost all the clothes I buy are from Bloomingdales. Hugo Boss is my other favorite brand. Their clothes just fit me so well. Even their T-shirts are a steal for like $80 to a $100.

I wouldn't say a steal because they're T-shirts, but they fit better than any of the regular T-shirts I buy. I don't know why. Maybe it is the brand, but it seems like they fit better.

What's interesting is clothes at Hugo Boss or Bloomingdales never go on sale. But that's the exception to the rule because clothes at most department sales are always on sale.

You see, it's the sales that drive the sales. Putting things on sale makes people buy more because people want a deal.

So, having a big sale is just a great way to generate a bunch of cash flow, especially for a business that's in a tricky situation.

If it's a business that's in a dire situation they're struggling to pay their bills and now they're hiring you for $10,000 or $25,000 (or for $2,000 a month, or $5,000 a month), then we need to help them make money fast.

A big sale could be a huge way to make big money fast.

Fast Money Strategy #5: Raise Your Prices

Most people are drastically under charging for their services, and they don't even know it.
So get your business owner clients to raise their prices.

And, before they raise their prices on current clients, start by charging the new customers the new rate.

Also tell them to grandfather in the current clients.

They don't want to create a mass exodus on all their clients by doubling their fees for the ones who are already paying them.

Don't bite the hand that feeds.

Also, make sure that you take good care of them.
If they're on a contract, for example, they signed up for a year at a $1,000 a month, and now their new clients are $2,000 a month, I wouldn't raise the current clients to $2,000 a month.

Make sure they honor the original contract.

And even afterwards, maybe they're not charging $3,000 a month yet, they can say: "Hey, if you want to keep working with me, let's meet in the middle."

And once there are enough new clients at the new rates, then they can raise their rates to existing clients.

Further, announcing an upcoming price increase can create a rush of sales, too. Just like having a sale, but without lowering the price.

Here's an example:

I remember when we were selling one of my online training programs.

We were selling it for $500 at the time, and we were going to raise it to a

$1,000. And I remember people were getting mad.

This one guy was mad at me and said, "Why are you raising the price?"

And I said, "Well, you don't have to pay more. You can just pay the regular price right now, but I think it's worth it."

And I doubled the price, and I doubled it again.

And I even sold it for 10x that original price, which wasn't the original price, but it was the price that he knew about at the time.

The bottom line is this: it's awesome to raise your fees.

It can lead to an immediate cashflow boost in your business.

One of the first things I do when clients hire me, is I say, "Charge more, let's see what happens."

It pushes buttons, and people are scared.

But if they're paying me a lot, they're a lot more likely to try it out.

I would say most clients who work with me start getting clients right away.

Here's A Recap Of The 5 Strategies:

1. Do more of what's working best
2. Re-activate past clients and customers
3. Go back to what's worked great in the past
4. Have a big sale
5. Raise your fees

Now, these "Fast Money" strategies are going to help your business clients make fast money, and some of them may apply to you and your business.

For example, if you don't have any strategies that used to work in the past because you're new, you can still do some of the other strategies.

But, these things are geared to make sure your business owner clients make money fast.

Now, not all of them need to make big money fast, right?

So, that's okay, too.

You don't have to do these with your clients. And you're going to want to know when to implement these strategies.

Because there will be times when it's good to help them make money fast, and when it's more important to keep your eyes on the long term game.

CONCLUSION

I've been coaching for 18+ years, and have seen trends in this industry come and go.

But I've never seen or experienced an opportunity in this industry as big or real as business coaching.
Coaching business owners has been a major factor in me creating a company that pulls in $5,000,000+ a year – starting from nothing.

And when you implement these secrets and create value for your business owner clients, you really have an opportunity of a lifetime to create the business of your dreams, and to do it fast.

You get to do work that you love, that actually makes a difference.

And it's work that you'll be appreciated for, recognized for, and paid handsomely for.

The bottom line is that if you want to be a business coach, you can be one and you can make a lot of money doing it and have an incredible life at the same time.

This book will give you a head start at making all your dreams come true.

But you need to be able to effectively help business owners with sales, marketing, leadership, team building, and their mindset.

And you need to know how to get business owner clients.

You need to know what to say and do, to get in front of more clients, how to get those stream of prospects coming in, and what to say during your intro-sessions to get clients to sign-up right on the spot.

You need to know how to talk to business owners, to get them to buy from you, and how to differentiate yourself from life coaches and other business coaches.

Now, how do you show up as a business coach so people take you seriously?
I used to think it was all about wearing a suit, and growing a beard when I was 25. I thought, "That's how I want to look as a business coach."

And certainly there's nothing wrong with that, but there's a lot more to showing up as a business coach than that

And then, there's how do you get them to sign-up with you right on the spot?

These are all important questions to answer.

Plus if you're already a high-paid business coach, you have to know how to get even more business owner clients, and how to be able to help them even more effectively.

These are all the things I teach, in-depth, inside the Big Money Business Coach Training And Certification Program.

And we take it one step further because, not only can all of these things help you grow your business...

...but we also have industry specific trainings for coaches who coach business owners.

You'll also get lots of forms, templates, and manuals that can help you become a Big Money Business Coach.

I'll be sharing details of the Big Money Business Coach program in my next video.

Remember, you are infinitely powerful!

BUSINESS COACH SECRETS

There are 27.9 million small business owners in the United States alone, and the vast majority of them need a coach who's skilled in the area of business coaching. Inside Business Coach Secrets you'll discover how to get and coach business owner clients no matter your level of experience.

Here's some of what you'll discover inside this book...
- 3 steps for getting business owner clients
- The 4 levels of value you can create for business clients
- The keys to becoming a Big Money Business Coach and 5 strategies that'll help your clients make big money fast
- Secrets to make big money as a business coach
- How to access the Business Coach Training and Certification Program
- And so much more...

Many people think they need years of business experience or that you need to be a superstar business owner with an incredible track record in order to help business owners. Nothing could be further from the truth and I'll show you the exact systems and processes you need in order to succeed in this highly profitable niche. I can't wait for you to dive into this book and discover how to get and coach high-paying business owner clients!

ABOUT THE AUTHOR

Christian Mickelsen is a leading authority on personal development and personal coaching and is the author of 5 number one best-selling books:
- Abundance Unleashed: Open Yourself To More Money, Love, Health, And Happiness Now
- How to Quickly Get Started As a Personal Coach: Make Great Money Changing People's Lives
- Change The World And Make Great Money Teaching, Training and Serving Humanity
- Get Clients Today: How to Get a Surge of New, High-Paying Coaching Clients Today and Every Day

He's the owner of a multi-million dollar coaching business that has made the Inc. 5000 list of fastest growing companies 4 years in a row. He's been featured in Forbes, Yahoo Finance, and MSN, among others. A true visionary, and pioneering personal coach for over 18 years, he's helped hundreds of thousands around the world experience the life-changing power of coaching. He's on a mission to get the whole world coached. He lives in San Diego with his wife and three daughters.

CHRISTIANMICKELSEN.COM

Made in the USA
Middletown, DE
01 May 2021